OMANIA]

m the French

nd -manie.

on of one's

ntal prowess,

er; madness;

andeur.

MEGALOMANIA

Too Much Is Never Enough

© 2008 Assouline Publishing
601 West 26th Street, 18th Floor
New York, NY 10001 USA
Tel.: 212-989-6810 Fax: 212-647-0005
www.assouline.com

Translated from French by Linda Jarosiewicz

ISBN: 978 2 84323 894 9

Printed in China

PHILIPPE TRÉTIACK

MEGALOMANIA

Too Much Is Never Enough

ASSOULINE

Here lies Saadat Hasan Manto, and with him, the art and mystery of the short story.
He is buried beneath layers of earth, forever wondering if it is he
or God who is the master of the short story.

SAADAT HASAN MANTO
Epitaph composed by the Urdu writer for himself (he died in 1955 in Lahore, Pakistan,
where he'd fled to after being devastated by the partition
of India and Pakistan).

To defy the years, to build for the centuries, to construct to endure; to fashion the horizon for coming generations, to imagine the world as a river whose shores you are forming; to take both natural disasters and riots in stride. To believe yourself a demiurge, more eternal than wars, than schisms, than revolutions. To crush fellow humans, to engrave your name on the sides of mountains, to erect statues and palaces, to launch fleets of airplanes emblazoned with your signature, your logo, your face. To be first; to speak loudest; to show off, to embrace vulgarity, to flaunt your bankroll and throw your money around; to dazzle with the glitter of diamonds, crying "Me! Me! I know!" Me alone. To be on a first-name basis with God. To be no more than your own overdeveloped ego; to become drunk with narcissism…
To be a megalomaniac.

Megalomania is universal, timeless, always contemporary. To it we owe bad habits, conflicts, and massacres but also small islands of extravagant bliss, corners of paradise, masterpieces, poems and monuments, songs and laments. Among the best: the Pyramids of Egypt, the Great Wall of China, the statues on Easter Island, the dolmens of Stonehenge, the temple of Angkor Wat, the Taj Mahal, the Hall of Mirrors at Versailles, the slender turrets of the castle built by King Ludwig II of Bavaria, and the Eiffel Tower. Further down the list are the eagle's nest of Adolf Hitler, the overblown palace of Nicolae Ceausescu, and the gigantic statues of Lenin, Hitler, Mao, and Kim Il-sung. To it we owe the self-named skyscrapers standing like totems and the cities that have sprung up whole, right in the middle of nowhere. Yesterday Brasília; tomorrow Astana, in Kazakhstan, and Pyinmana, in Myanmar; and today, Dubai, a multicultural city in the United Arab Emirates, where more than a hundred nationalities live together in defiance of the climate by virtue of air-conditioning. Architecture, an art of excess in which erection is second nature, is at base a phallic assertion. High on technical innovation, engineers play with mad inspiration, cantilevers worthy of Damocles tensed on the edge of a void and skyscrapers in the thousands of feet. Among them are the Petronas Twin Towers in Kuala Lumpur, Jin Mao in Shanghai, the Sears Tower in Chicago, the Taipei 101 tower, and Burj Dubai, for now the tallest tower under construction in the world, at nearly half a mile high—these spires of glass and steel thrust themselves heavenward, snubbing the laws of gravity. Risks taken throughout the world have made the fame of architects such as Piano, Foster, Pei, Calatrava, Koolhaas, Nouvel, Ito—and their financiers. Higher, taller, always bigger! Each additional floor is a new salvo fired at their challengers. Where will it end? In the eleventh century, San Gimignano, in Italy, saw hubristic, lopsided, narrow ziggurats sprout from its Tuscan soil. How many are left? The ancient city of Bagan, in Myanmar, dissolved in a quarrel over stupas, each one larger and more costly than the last. The sands have long since covered them. But no matter. Other megalomaniacs rise to take their place, drunk on records and fame.

Megalomania is a recorded psychiatric illness that consists of overestimating one's abilities. Those afflicted by it become prowlers of asylums, clients of the men and women in white coats. Like a racing locomotive with its wheels burning up the rails, megalomania translates into an immoderate desire for power, the projected version of an irresistible love of self. In psychiatry, this illness is classed in the family of chronic delirious psychoses. It should not surprise, then, that from the hands of those megalomaniacs spring aggressive villas, palaces festooned with Jacuzzis, pinnacles of Romanesque splendor, decadent, extravagant, orgiastic. The Burj Al Arab (the Tower of the Arabs), in Dubai, designed to look like a billowing sail and decked out with schmaltzy, fluorescent colors, is the only hotel in the world that promotes itself as a seven-star establishment. Or there is the Playboy Mansion of Hugh Hefner, manliest of men, where he splashes about in the pool, covered with statuesque naiads. Let it be said: Megalomania satisfies the senses. Its urges are orders. Nourished by grandiose visions, it devours. It is Julius Caesar without end. And never mind if the marble civilizations finish by crumbling. Megalomaniacs believe they are eternal.

All builders are megalomaniacs; all architecture is a form of megalomania. Those who seek to live on beyond their own existence see themselves as empire builders. They aim their sights high. But their marble works, unchanging and exalted, will one day be their cenotaphs. Nero met his end by burning down Rome. After me, the flood.

Star architects, from Francesco Borromini to Frank Gehry, are all autocrats, men of iron dipped in the steel of brutal resolution, sprung from stone quarries, designed to resist in the face of adversity, to never submit, and to stand right to the end. Worlds were erected based on their visions. Opponents were broken. More than one builder has paid dearly for these excesses: the Millennium Dome in London, doomed to scandal; Egypt's Aswan Dam, with its disastrous ecological consequences. There are costs to be borne. Alas, how many have placed their visionary talent in the service of bloodthirsty tyrants? Nazi officials promised an inviolable Third Reich. Hermann Goering reportedly vowed that no enemy plane would fly over Berlin for a thousand years. Albert Speer, Adolf Hitler's beloved architect, became this nightmare's town planner. He designed a capital, not for Germany alone, but for the empire of the swastika. Speer draped his all-concrete stadium at Nuremberg with red-and-black banners like blossoms, propaganda carried on the wind. Designed to mimic the Doric architecture of the Great Altar of Pergamon, but enlarged to gigantic proportions, this stadium could welcome 240,000 people. At the Nazis' rally there in 1934, Speer placed one hundred and fifty antiaircraft searchlights around the site, commandeering the night sky itself and creating,

in the words of British ambassador Neville Henderson, a "cathedral of light."
Speer demonstrated all the morbid power of megalomania in a minimum
amount of time. He constructed a theory of *Ruinenwert*, or ruin value, for Hitler:
Within a thousand years, all of the Reich's buildings would transform
themselves into ruins as magnificent as those of the temples of ancient Greece.
Megalomania always flirts with the morbid. It is *vanitas*, writ large.
Karl Marx wrote that history repeats itself, first as a tragedy, then as a farce.
The construction of the Notre Dame de la Paix basilica, an inflated replica
of Rome's Saint Peter's Basilica, in Yamoussoukro, Ivory Coast, in the 1980s,
confirms this. Félix Houphouët-Boigny, the country's president and great builder,
wanted the basilica to have seven thousand seats and as many individual air-
conditioning systems. Constructed in the heart of the village where he was born,
the building sticks out like a sore thumb. The small town, suddenly thrust into the
limelight as the administrative capital in place of Abidjan, is doing its utmost to
fight the heat and decay, but Africa sets its conditions, and this megalomaniacal
buffoonery is being consumed by the fire of the sun. A failure following on the
heels of so many others! Built by Emperor Akbar, in Uttar Pradesh, in 1569,
Fatehpur Sikri was abandoned only thirteen years later, vanquished by dryness.
Only a ghost town remains, an echo of Mughal delusions.
More recently, in the very heart of Europe, Nicolae Ceausescu, the Romanian
Conductor, the "Genius of the Carpathians," built himself a palace in Bucharest
that was as ugly as it was extreme. His neoclassical style, as heavy as if erected
from crushed tanks, with its stiff columns like soldiers impersonating Byzantine
porticoes, shocks with its hideousness. Within its interminable corridors,
the wall coverings broke records for length and width. These derisory
accomplishments probably required legions of workers to realize. And who
knows? Perhaps they were even proud of their modest contribution to the
magnificence of this regime that made daily life so miserable. The decor soon

became as dull and dusty as the dictator's repressive state. To build his new city, Ceausescu destroyed entire districts of old Bucharest. Palaces, villas, churches, taverns, workshops, and hovels all fell beneath the onslaught of his mechanical shovels. Existing streets were bulldozed and straightened to accommodate his tracked vehicles. As a result, the city was invaded by dogs, whose owners, chased from their old homes, did not want to shut them up in the new towers, already being eaten by rust. There were soon 300,000 hungry canines roaming the dark streets. And Bucharest became the city of dog bites.

As early as 1925, Le Corbusier designed his Plan Voisin for Paris, which called for the heart of the capital to be bulldozed and replaced by a district of skyscrapers arranged like wooden blocks. Fortunately, his city-destroying project was stopped in time. But others have taken up Corbusier's torch. During the past ten years, China has razed 93 percent of its ancient cities, in Beijing as well as in Suzhou, the Chinese Venice. Yesterday, the hammer and sickle; today, the pneumatic drill, all for the greater glory of the party leaders. The East laid claim to Red.

The Soviets designed palaces for their people. The Moscow metro—and to a lesser extent those in Kiev, Ukraine, and Belarus—overflows with gilt, chandeliers, and heroic bas-reliefs. This great pandemonium of statues, mosaics, and commemorative plaques oozes gloom, like a first-class funeral— working class, of course. Set in deep underground tunnels to escape shelling, this proletarian strain of megalomania has the look of a crystal mole trap. In Moscow's Manege Square, within a stone's throw of the Kremlin, a shopping center of unbridled bad taste now fills the surface and underground of a previously empty and, for that reason, majestic square. Faced with the nauseating spread of faux marble and factory-wrought iron, filmmaker Federico Fellini reportedly let slip, "It looks like it was designed by a drunk pastry cook." Megalomaniacs always grab the largest share of the cake.

"Too much is never enough" was the motto of Morris Lapidus, the American architect who revolutionized Miami's Art Deco tranquility. He constructed the Fontainebleau Hotel in an ultra-kitschy style combining Versailles gold and Chantilly cream, shaking up the seaside torpor. Its useless staircases, immense chandeliers, and theatrical pomp gratified the promoters and seduced the clientele. Lapidus gave middle-class America a pedestal so that retired vacationers could, for an instant, imagine themselves Oscar winners or tycoons the equal of a Rockefeller or Howard Hughes.

Bad taste is the escutcheon of excessive architecture. Look at Las Vegas and its palaces: the New York, the Paris with its Eiffel Tower, the Venetian, whose one-third scale campanile looks down on tourists from its fake bricks. And what can be said about the Grand Canal re-created on the first floor? "Gorgeous," shout the gondoliers, just in from Kansas or Michigan. But this is nothing compared with the Luxor and its pyramids, the Excalibur with its dungeons, the Mandalay Bay and its Buddhas. It is a modern mysticism that, in this era of globalization, wants to be able to make a world tour, slipping from an ersatz Europe to a sham Asia. Megalomania seeks to reduce the planet to a single strip, accessible within twenty-four hours from a moving sidewalk. Across the globe, again in Dubai, the Jumeirah Hotel complex rolls out 2.3 miles of fake Venetian canals. (It seems that every megalomaniac owes it to himself to erect his own Bridge of Sighs.) It is flanked by an ancient souk, also born yesterday, and in the lobby, five thousand roses are changed daily. A $140,000 Swarovski crystal chandelier hovers above the guests. "It's my favorite," exclaims the public relations officer uncorking Champagne. The jet-set lifestyle and megalomania go hand in hand. Jesus said to his disciple, "You are Peter, and on this rock, I will build my church." Zealots of the religion of leisure have taken him at his word and have set about building mirages in the desert. Of all languages, Babel is the most universal, and megalomania is its translation.

None of this, however, would exist without diktats, Neronian choices, wills of iron. At the highest levels of unbridled power we find not only the best entrepreneurs but also the worst autocrats. For the best, and first, the worst: Idi Amin Dada and his swimming pool swarming with crocodiles; Jean-Bédel Bokassa, crowned Emperor Bokassa the First of Central Africa, so dubbed by cheering cohorts. Later deposed, having found refuge in a decrepit château in France, the Napoleon of the equatorial forests clung to his former glory. When he received visitors, he would order one of his many sons to mount a moped and go in quest of a bottle of bubbly at the local convenience store. The revolutionary Lenin rode around in a Rolls Royce; Mao felt entitled to his pick of very young girls. Like Ho Chi Minh, these leaders were mummified and turned into holy relics of communism, megalomaniacs even in death. Since then, there have been the Mugabes, the Chávezes, the Castros, the Qadhafis, the Mubaraks, the Assads: All false gods, they are satraps who behave like sultans, christening boulevards, airports, and cities with their names. They can be found hoisted high on pedestals at crossroads, displayed on palace walls, showing the way, grabbing hold of the universe and the future in a delirium of self-love, striking their profile on coins as they strike their people with truncheons. A megalomaniacal dictator is an advertising executive with one client: He is the only brand he promotes until it swells and collapses. Propagandist without equal, Venezuelan president Hugo Chávez is on the air every Sunday, omnipresent on every channel. For hours, he talks about the imperialist plot against his country as matter-of-factly as if he were talking about watering plants. Omniscient, he controls everything. Saddam Hussein, dreaming himself the equal and even the rival of the great conquerors, Alexander, Attila, Bolívar… Did he not vow, on January 17, 2002, to fight the "mother of all battles"?

Kings, emperors, overlords, artists, gurus—there is a long list of practitioners of megalomania. All the leaders of parties, clans, and tribes; Mafia kingpins; Colombian drug lords; the clandestine heads of Chinese triads surrounded by dimwitted thugs and call girls drowning in diamonds and jewels. And let's not forget the tycoons, all the lucky devils on Wall Street, the ones whose names have become a trademark displayed in all four corners of the world, those whose fame is dispatched everywhere by myriad trucks and planes, begging to be branded megalomaniacs. With their unimpeded cash flows, they dip into the adults' toy box: Rolls, Bentley, Ferrari, Porsche, private jet, yacht, helicopter, telephone encrusted with jewels, the special-order Vuitton bag in monogrammed pistachio-green ostrich, unique and unequaled, everything private and exclusive, the passport of the elite. Their escapades warp their closet doors—think of Imelda Marcos and her thousands of pairs of shoes; Eva Perón and her drawers overflowing with lingerie. Her opponents put it on display to discredit her, but her admirers only adored her all the more.

And they are not the only ones. Like the Reverend Jim Jones urging his faithful followers by the hundred to suicide in Guyana in 1978, others are following hard on their heels: gurus with their hypnotic gibberish; forgers; Scientologists; turbaned leaders of esoteric sects or schools; prophets of the apocalypse; miraculous healers; pseudo-discoverers of brilliant therapies and cures for depression, cancer—and megalomania! There are swarms of televangelists able to transform churches into giant karaoke bars, all these enthusiastic preachers of a Theology of Prosperity that authorizes them to develop their instincts, their excesses, diamond-studded rings on all ten fingers, glittering tiepins. They are here, there, everywhere. Megalomania is an epidemic.
Ah, to bring the masses together, subjugate them, tame them, galvanize them into action! Stars of rock, rap, hip-hop, pop, and punk, the divas burning out in public,

thrown alive into the flames of hysteria, are showing the way. Look at them: Sinatra; Madonna; Mick Jagger; the Beatles ("more popular than Jesus"); Bruce Springsteen, called the Boss; James Brown, the eternal sex machine, convinced he had invented every dance: the jerk, the Madison, the smurf. Celine Dion, a small, fragile Quebecois singer, went on to become the Callas of the megatour. So yes, smile to show off the diamonds stuck in your teeth; snigger with the rappers—millionaires at sixteen, dead at eighteen on the strip in Vegas, killed in a drive-by shooting and immediately lionized. Cross the ghetto with them, slowly, in a Dodge Viper convertible riding low on gleaming wheels. Cruise enemy territory, propelled by a throbbing bass beat, a total provocation and a maximum risk. The megalomaniac thinks he is invincible. He is wrong. All the same, he wears his solid-gold slave's chain, flaunting it like an act of revenge, and packs a revolver with a mother-of-pearl grip, thinking himself a majestic, heroic pimp. Bling is to the megalomaniac like the final glaze on a superstretch Hummer, a glint, a brilliance that cuts through the dark like a gunshot.

Yes, this is show business: an ultravixen with gigantic breasts, more woman than other women, a top model; a telegenic Italian prime minister with a facelift; a media mogul with a dazzling smile, showing a minimum of sixty-four teeth. The explosion of celebrity magazines has given megalomania a boost it hardly needed. Everyone can have his or her fifteen minutes of fame with a romance, a breakup, an accident, or a trip to the grocery store. All their actions scream "Look at me!" In Moscow, "protectors" stake out nightclubs, pushing aside bunches of girls in G-strings to sit down and arrange their six cell phones on the low tables. In New Delhi, in the beautiful restaurant at the Imperial hotel, a show-off strolled around with two cell phones at a time when they were still rare, probably calling himself from one to the other. Wherever they go, megalomaniacs are always onstage, obsessed with being looked at, basking in admiration filtered through their love of self.

Megalomania has an attitude and a look: the chest thrown out; a haughty, piercing gaze; a sure step. Pro athletes know it well, with their strong, swaggering bodies, raised on a stepping-stone of muscle to reach new heights of wealth and excess. The body is always at the heart of megalomania. Self-consumption soon shades into cannibalism. Fashion designers reproduce their anorexic silhouettes or their ultrabronzed features. The French artist Sophie Calle puts her daily life on display in her artwork; Orlan makes her body her canvas with surgeries and implants; Pete Doherty is still tampering with his already abused body in an attempt to paint and sculpt his own legend—not to mention all the others who want to sign their names on the universe.
Their ambition? To become a hero. To be a superman, the star of their own saga. To roar like the Metro-Goldwyn-Mayer lion.

Our era has given itself free rein, and megalomania is boiling over.
Look at these sportsmen and women who are conquerors of the pointless.
Not content to climb the north face or the south face of this mountain
or that glacier, they want to do it ever faster, to beat all the records.
They plant their names as they would plant a flag on the oxygen-deprived peaks of the Andes, Anapurna, Mont Blanc—once, ten times, a hundred times. Go further, go faster; slide into a steel fuselage and fire up the thrusters, risking total disintegration of the sheet metal, prelude to an explosion of the body. Yesterday, Christopher Columbus conquered America; Attila swept across Europe; and Livingstone searched for the sources of the Nile. Today's mountaineer is a windsurfer dropped by helicopter on waves sixty-five feet high. Megalomania is inscribed in the quest and in conquest. These days new frontiers are found not at the edges of the Earth but at the limits of science, and microtechnology has opened up a new playground for megalomaniacs.

Today technology has become a will to technology, in the Nietzschean sense. Science has gotten away from us, and our tragedies have changed in scope as well as in nature. Technological megalomania gave birth to the atom bomb, with its capacity for total destruction. Hiroshima, Nagasaki, Chernobyl. Everywhere, the will to power flirts with catastrophe. It is Babel again and always repeated. For every erection foreshadows a collapse; every invention produces its opposite. To be born is to start to die. In this race to cheat death, biologists and scientists have become the new puppeteers of the universe. Shaking the test tube, they triturate the DNA helix, take apart the causal chain, cherish the clone, and imagine themselves to be God Almighty. Clinical megalomania is overflowing in the laboratories, escaping from its masters, while anonymous megalomaniacs are rebraiding the very fiber of life. What will the end result be? A generation of humans with the resistance of titanium, their powers increased tenfold? In the future, will everyone be a megalomaniac? We will have to conceal it from one another, to differentiate ourselves, to become even stronger, more famous, and precisely for that reason, be forced to disappear. What, then, will be the showiest display? The 4x4 with the tinted windows, symbol of the power of the person you can't see, who has withdrawn from the world, forced by his own fame into reclusion—still a man, but already a god. Megalomania is a passport to the beyond.

Following pages:
The cult of personality raised to an art form: what communism does best. Perhaps only the pomp of the Vatican can rival this avalanche of gold and scarlet devoted to Mao Tse-tung. Alas, behind the glory and the thoughts of "the Great Helmsman" is hidden the savage reality of the 50 to 70 million Chinese who died under Communist rule in peacetime.

Previous pages:
The interior of Romanian dictator Nicolae Ceausescu's palace, with windows that reach thirty feet high.
When Ceausescu fell in 1989, construction of the palace was only 70 percent complete. Work is currently in progress.

Above:
Napoleon I on His Imperial Throne, Jean-Auguste-Dominique Ingres, 1806. More than any other conqueror,
Napoleon Bonaparte symbolizes the splendor of personal omnipotence. Heir of the Roman emperors in spirit
and in mien, he was an ideal subject for painters. His conquests, his victories, and, in the end, his dethronement
and exile have burnished his image. A simple life became a destiny, and finally a myth.

Opposite:
Rapper Jay-Z on a throne, 2002. Gold slave chains around their necks, diamonds in their teeth and ears,
platinum piercings, rings on every finger, up to their ears in top models: rappers have willingly adopted
an in-your-face look; they are the nouveau riche, embracing vulgarity. Success is expressed through
its external symbols. The throne is only the beginning.

Previous pages:
An American helicopter flies over one of the
four busts of Saddam Hussein in Baghdad,
December 2, 2003. That very night, these
symbols of authoritarian power were lifted from
their pedestals and carried out of public view.

Opposite:
The basilica of Notre Dame de la Paix
in Yamoussoukro, Ivory Coast. President
Félix Houphouët-Boigny conceived, and in
1989, revealed his replica of Saint Peter's
Basilica in Rome, equipped with a sophisticated
air-conditioning system. An echo of the Vatican
in the middle of nowhere, the project's incon-
gruity stems from the void that surrounds it.

31

Opposite:
The Monument to Victor Emmanuel II, in Milan's Piazza del Duomo, wrapped by Christo and Jeanne-Claude in 1970. Every monument pays tribute to a dream of bygone glory. It freezes the past, emphasizing its morbidity. The coverings with which Christo has decked out various urban showpieces, such as the Reichstag in Berlin or the Pont Neuf in Paris, highlight this fact with all the magnificence of funerary drapes. And yet, is not attacking these giant works, blinding them and making them disappear the ultimate in artistic megalomania?

Following pages:
Palm Island, Dubai. Jet-setters, this is for you, for all the architecture on this affluent islet, which stretches out into the Persian Gulf, can only be truly appreciated from an airplane. From the sky, the form of a palm tree reveals itself on the sea. The small island's luxury villas have all found buyers.

Previous pages:
The Badaling section of the Great Wall of China, to the north of Beijing. To be locked in, to contain foreign influences, to keep from being soiled by others: Here is the condensed version of the megalomaniacal dream of autarky applied to an entire people by its emperor. Legend has it that the Great Wall, 4,163 miles long, is the only human monument visible from outer space. This is false.

Opposite:
The Sol de Occidente villa on the Costa Careyes in Mexico. The style of the Italian architect Gian Franco Brignone characterizes the Costa Careyes in the state of Jalisco, on Mexico's western shore. His luxury creations are dotted along the section of coast that he owns. Eco-friendly and refined, the palm roofs and adobe walls are a good substitute for air-conditioning. Clinging to the side of the cliff, the pink Occidente, encircled by a pool, and its sister, the Sol de Oriente, bedecked in yellow, stand as sentinels on either side of the bay. This steep hillside, suspended between the Pacific Ocean and the tropical forest, has become the new promised land for a handful of the fabulously wealthy.

Proſpect vom Babylonischen Thurm.

Ioh: Georg Schmidt Sculp.

This page:
An imaginary reconstruction of the Tower of Babel by Johann Georg Schmidt in the eighteenth century. Started by men who wanted to reach God in heaven, this tower mentioned in the biblical book of Genesis is the focal point of all of humanity's dreams of grandeur. We know how the story ended—with the proliferation of languages and general confusion.

Opposite:
Construction of the Burj Dubai tower. Builders of skyscrapers are engaging in all-out war in the race for records. The United Arab Emirates city should be able to boast of having the tallest in the world for some time, though, as the Burj Dubai should reach nearly half a mile high. Its precise height is being kept secret, for fear of rival projects.

Above:
The crowd of spectators saluting the arrival of the Führer during the Berlin Olympic Games in 1936.
Albert Speer, Adolf Hitler's architect, designed all the Third Reich's buildings as part of the propaganda campaign
to magnify the presence of the leader and the animal force of the crowds he electrified.

Opposite:
In 1934, Speer transformed the Nuremberg stadium into a "cathedral of light" using one hundred and fifty
antiaircraft searchlights and enlivened the raw concrete with billowing flags emblazoned with black swastikas.
These references to ancient ceremonies reinforced the idea of a new empire being formed, a German empire.

Following pages:
The Hall of Mirrors at Versailles. Until the middle of the nineteenth century, mirrors were a rarity. The expertise
of Italian glass artisans was long a state secret, and revealing it to foreigners was punishable by death. Therefore,
people came from afar to see this gallery of four hundred mirrors that contested the supremacy of Venetian glassmakers.
People also came to gaze at their own reflections, as if the power of these mirrors was somehow echoed in them.

A still from the film *Intolerance*, by D. W. Griffith, 1916. By interweaving three epochal melodramas—the fall of Babylon, the Crucifixion of Christ, and the Saint Bartholomew's Day Massacre—with a contemporary story line, Griffith, the renowned filmmaker whose credits include *Birth of a Nation,* a much lauded but racist film, wanted to create an epic work. He emerged battered and in debt, as if the subject of downfall, in its various guises, had ensnared him. The film remains a monument of grandiose images.

Previous page, left to right:
The Russia Tower, conceived by architect Norman Foster. Two thousand vertical feet host offices, a hotel, cultural facilities, and private residences perched high in the sky. It is situated within Moscow's new 247-acre financial district, Moskva City, complete with gleaming metal skyscrapers—a feat, for the Russian capital is built on flaky soil. Nature will thus be obliged to bow to the demands of its directors! Megalomania and Mother Russia go hand in hand.

Plan for the World Financial Center, Shanghai, China, 2005. The tallest skyscraper in China at one hundred and one stories, the World Financial Center tears the title of record height from the neighboring Jin Mao Tower. Side by side, these two buildings form a remarkable pair in the skyline of Pudong, the new district of the coastal city. Nicknamed the "bottle opener" because of the rectangular opening at its peak, the original design of the tower called for a round hole, but the Chinese authorities protested—they saw it as an allusion to the Japanese flag. Scheduled for completion in November 2008, the skyscraper includes offices, a five-star hotel, restaurants, spas, and, of course, the most breathtaking views in Shanghai.

Plan for the Chicago Spire (formerly known as Fordham Spire), 2005. This building, designed by architect Santiago Calatrava, is destined to be the tallest skyscraper in the United States. Like many projects across the globe, the tower takes up the idea of the spiral, a formal conceptualization of perpetual movement. In a world of flux, architects attempt to imbue their static creations with the energy that typifies society as a whole. Even skyscrapers must be on the move, always going forward.

Plan for the Sumida Tower in Tokyo, Japan. Once completed in 2009, this structure will reach just over two thousand feet.

Opposite:
The western facade of Antonio Gaudí's Sagrada Familia cathedral. Wanting to be independent from Madrid, the government of Catalonia had the architect, a native son, construct a new style. He borrowed heavily from Viollet-le-Duc to revive the medieval era, the height of Catalan greatness. The cathedral designed by this pious man remained unfinished at his death, in 1926. Catalonia has since tried to complete its erection.

Above:
The lobby of the Hyatt Hotel as seen from the upper floors in the Jin Mao Tower in Shanghai.
The tallest skyscraper in the city was recently supplanted by its neighbor, the Shanghai World
Financial Center. The 1,381-foot-high Jin Mao overlooks the new district of Pudong.
Its design was inspired by traditional pagodas and symbolizes the dynamism of China's new society.

Opposite:
The 1993 Umeda Sky Building by Hiroshi Hara, in the Shin-Umeda district of Osaka, Japan.

Following pages:
Aerial view of Sun City, Arizona, 1992. Thanks to its radiant town planning, the windows of the homes
in this city, located in the middle of the desert, point toward its center. The community of forty-six
thousand is thus bound together by this common view. The pioneer mentality of the American West
is the law of the land. The determination of the entire community has triumphed over the rugged
environment that surrounds it.

Previous pages:
Muhammad Ali (born Cassius Clay), the former world heavyweight boxing champion, encapsulates human megalomania in its totality, expressing itself with fists and measuring its importance in liters of sweat. Agitator, braggart, rebel, actor, he strikes the pose of an indestructible King Kong on a Chicago bridge in 1996.

Above:
Project by the architects Vladimir Gelfreikh, Boris Iofan, Vladimir Shchuko, and the sculptor Sergei Merkurov for the Palace of Soviets, 1934. At the start of the 1930s, Stalin put a stop to the innovative architecture of the Constructivist period and demanded that builders return to a more grandiloquent style. Roman-inspired Soviet neoclassicism had arrived.

Opposite:
Mount Rushmore, chiseled with the effigies of four American presidents: George Washington, Thomas Jefferson, Theodore Roosevelt, and Abraham Lincoln. The sculptures are sixty feet tall. The "greats" of this world love to be shown beside these four colossal figures from American history. To be the fifth man (or woman) on Mount Rushmore will be a crowning achievement! Alfred Hitchcock set the final scene of his 1959 masterpiece *North by Northwest* on the heights of Mount Rushmore.

The warriors of Emperor Shi Huangdi's army, Shaanxi Province, China. Qin Shi Huang was the founder of the first imperial dynasty. He established, among other things, a penal system and organized the first "administration." He even claimed to possess the qualities of a deity. He had towers built in order to be in contact with the spirits and sent off marine expeditions in search of the immortal paradises. Most importantly, he launched the construction of the Great Wall. He died in 210 B.C. During his reign, he had a mausoleum built; measuring nearly two dozen square miles and watched over by an army of 7,000 unique terra-cotta soldiers, he mobilized more than 700,000 workers for its construction. Today some believe this monument should be added to the Seven Wonders of the World.

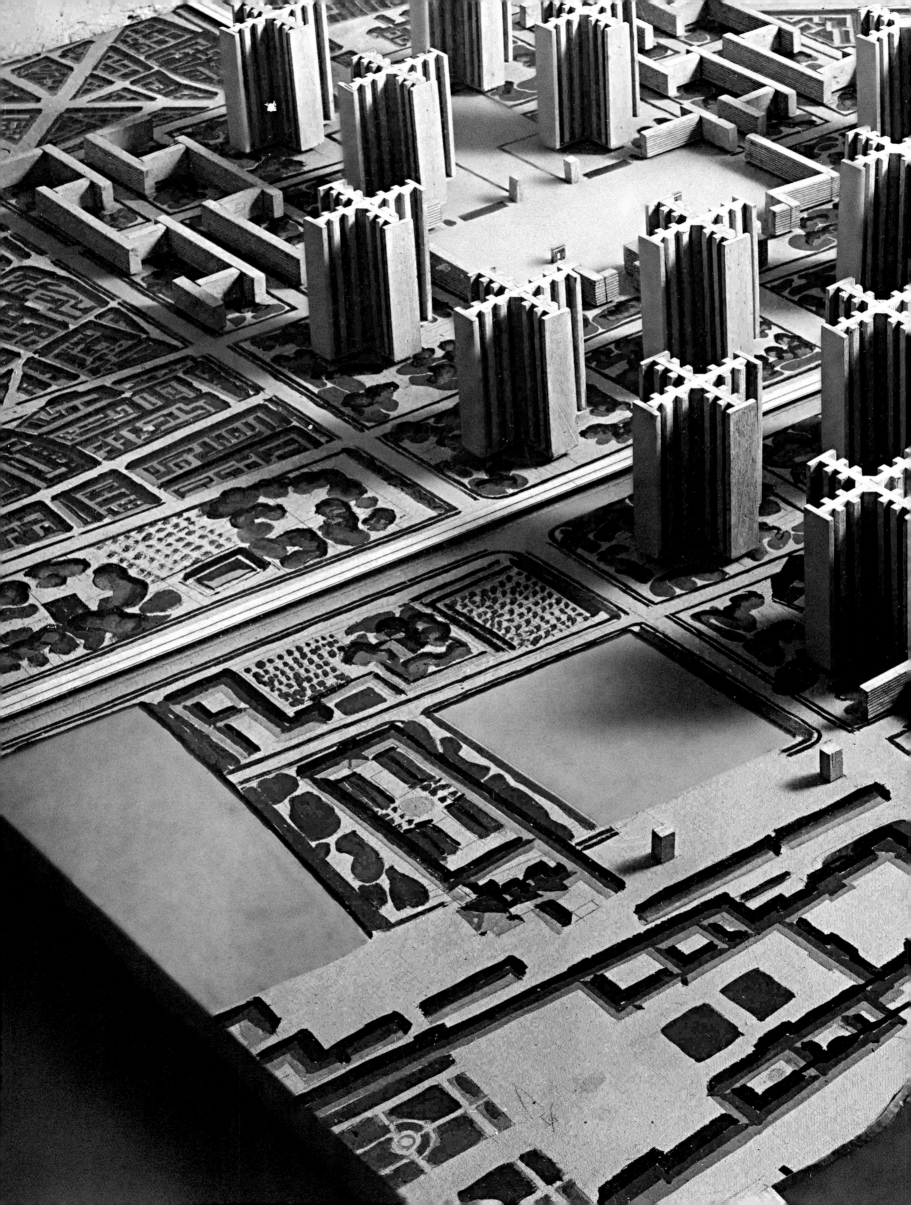

Previous pages:
Plan Voisin, by Le Corbusier, 1925. Convinced of the legitimacy of hygienist theories
and resolved to separate leisure and domestic activities from those relating to work,
Le Corbusier drew a radical redesign for the city of Paris. He suggested razing the city's central
section on the Right Bank and erecting a grid of towers in its place. Fortunately this vision
never became a reality—at least in France. Currently, China looks forward to the realization
of about ten similar plans in Beijing and elsewhere.

Opposite:
The interior of the Burj Al Arab in Dubai, the only hotel in the world that promotes itself
as a seven-star establishment. This sail dominating the sea has become the symbol of Dubai,
its Eiffel Tower. A helicopter landing pad on the roof, a tennis court cantilevered over the water,
and the assurance of having at least one international star present at all times makes it one
of the most popular spots with the jet set.

Following pages:
A choir sings under the portrait of former North Korean president Kim Il-sung. The state-imposed
aesthetic, with its kitschy crudeness, is becoming almost trendy among artists in other parts of the
world. Alas, in Pyongyang, symbols are not a joking matter. Everything is true, even false glory.

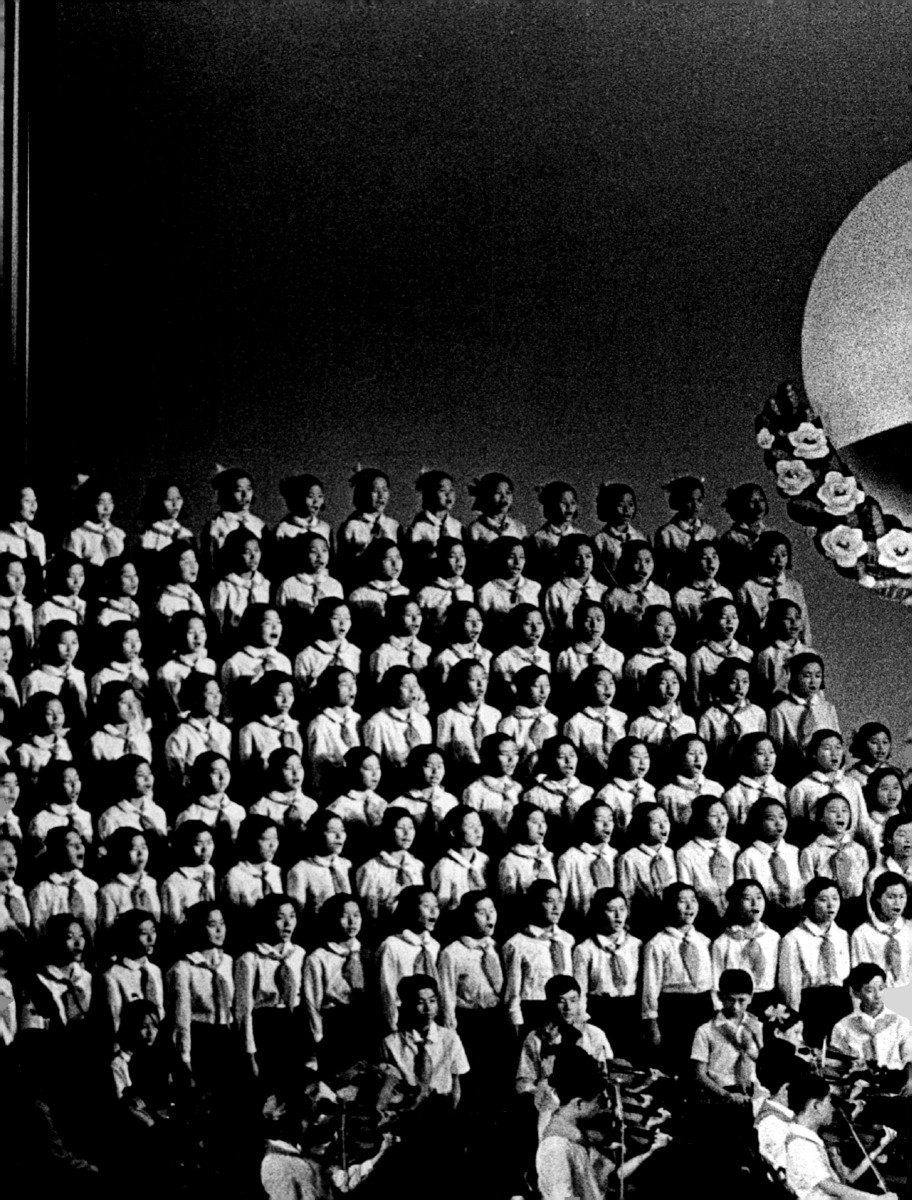

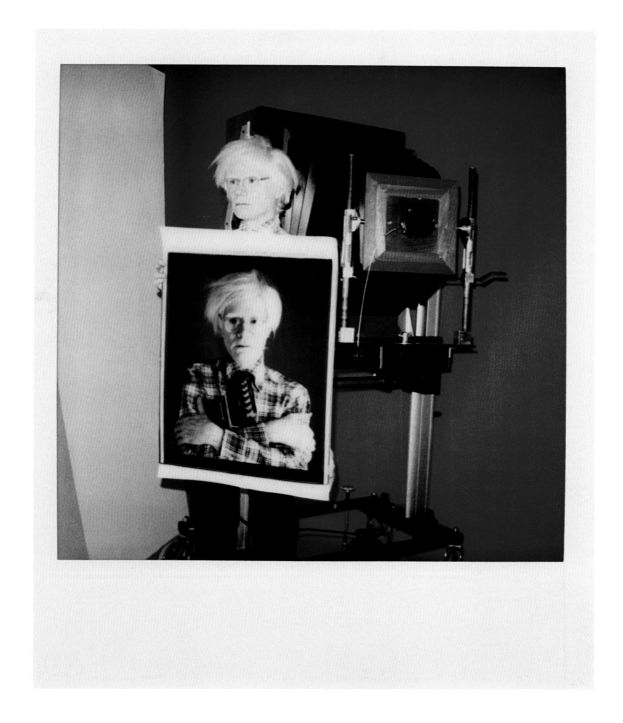

Above:
Self-portrait by Andy Warhol, 1975. An inspired creator and an outstanding communicator, he was the first to grasp that the artist would soon be more important than his or her art. Warhol staged his own stardom. He became a journalist, chief of the tribe, and used advertising, rock and roll, and experimental cinema to make his life an artistic creation.

Opposite:
Refiguration/Self-Hybridation No. 2, Orlan, 1998. The French artist, born in 1947, has made her appearance a work of art in perpetual evolution. Pioneer of body art, fan of silicone implants, Orlan is at once a champion of plastic surgery and its most hostile critic. With her surgical-operation performances, Orlan exacerbates human megalomania, embodied in this communal urge to slow the passage of time with cuts of the scalpel and Botox injections. In using her body as material for modeling, she demystifies it, and in exhibiting it as an artwork in progress, she mystifies it even more, bringing her viewers face-to-face with ambiguity.

Opposite:
Best in the West, a billboard by artist-
provocateur Patrick Mimran in New York's
Chelsea gallery district, February 2005.

Following pages:
Shanghai's famous Pudong skyline.
In ten years, China has destroyed
a considerable part of its cultural heritage.
Thousands of cranes are silhouetted against
its horizon, and work sites are everywhere,
devouring the world's steel output.
The Pudong skyline has become the symbol
of a march forward that will culminate
in the 2010 World's Fair.
Chinese power will then be at its peak.

Howard Hughes seated in his new airplane, the XF-11, July 1946. A powerful billionaire, a recluse, a pioneer of aviation and of cinema, a hit with Hollywood's leading ladies, a victim of mental troubles—Hughes was a legend in his own time. This larger-than-life figure was recently the subject of a feature-length film by Martin Scorsese, no stranger to epic stories.

The German artist Ingrid Webendoerfer imagined raising the Île de la Cité in Paris on a pedestal, a glacis of concrete.

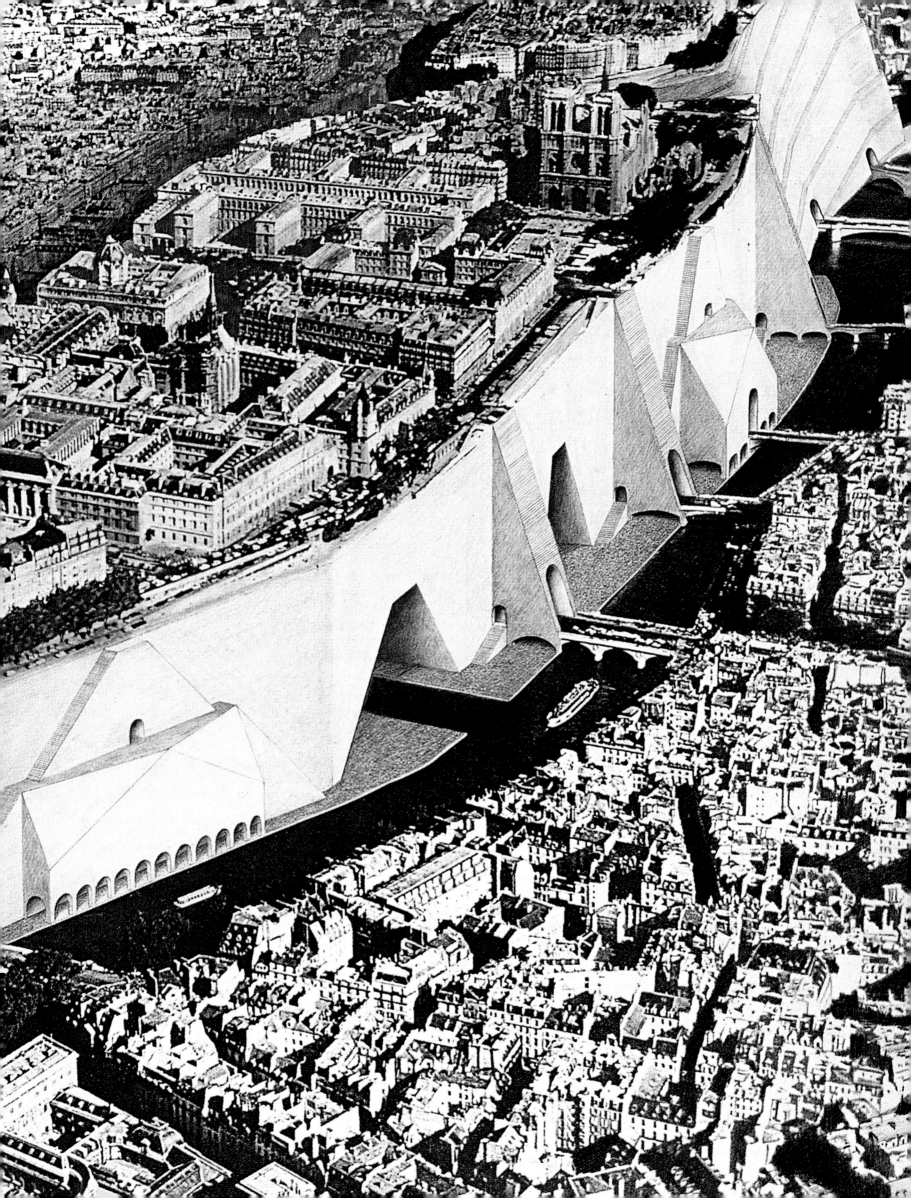

Opposite:
Statue of the former North Korean president Kim Il-sung, with the raised arm required of dictators. The chief, the guide, the beacon who shows the way and defies heaven. Every tyrant from the Roman emperors to Adolf Hitler has loved this haughty gesture. The people of North Korea may be dying of hunger, but they have a beautiful future ahead of them.

Following pages:
Two men painting the portrait of Venezuelan president Hugo Chávez. Propaganda is an integral part of political megalomania. In this case, Chávez is following in Lenin's footsteps—same gestures, same clothes, same revolutionary red background. It is identification as proof of reincarnation.

Above:
Hand of Mobutu Sese Seko Kuku Ngbendu Wa Za Banga (Mobutu the Warrior, Who Won Battle After Battle, Letting No One Stand in His Way), who ruled the Congo from 1965 to 1997. Proof of his autocratic willpower: he renamed it Zaire. A dictator eternally adorned with his leopard-skin toque, he was the archetypal African despot, who showed no mercy to his adversaries or any other opposition and who managed, all the while, to amass a considerable fortune abroad.

Opposite:
Jean-Bédel Bokassa during the parade organized for the twelfth anniversary of the Central African Republic, in 1970.

Following pages:
Palais de Justice (Palace of Justice) in Brussels, completed in 1883 by the architect Joseph Poelaert. It is thought to have been the largest public building in Europe until the construction of Ceausescu's palace in Bucharest, surpassed only by the Pentagon in the United States. This enormous neoclassical confection bears down heavily on those entering it for trial. The absurdity of its extravagant size gives it a surrealist air, which does not displease the Belgians.

Above:
Petronas Twin Towers in Kuala Lumpur, Malaysia, 1996. In the race for records, this double skyscraper, designed by Cesar Pelli, marks Malaysia's admission into the top group of successful Asian nations. These towers also boast some of the fastest elevators in the world. The cabins are pressurized to counter the devastating effects of acceleration.

Opposite:
Rockefeller Center, as seen from 444 Madison Avenue, in New York, photographed by Berenice Abbott, "Changing New York" series, 1937. With a name synonymous with fortune, the Rockefellers owed it to themselves to build a skyscraper in Manhattan. They went one better by also building a public urban space at the foot of their tower. Putting one's name on a building is the vertical version of having a street, an avenue, or a boulevard bear your name. A tower is a street that reaches for heaven.

This page:
Constantin Brancusi's *Endless Column* in Tirgu-Jiu, Romania, circa 1938.
The Romanian artist designed his sculpture as an ode to the infinite. Although anemic, it appears to go on forever. Its spiraling form also seems to disclose part of the mystery of DNA structure, which would not be modeled until 1953, when the scientists James Watson and Francis Crick revealed its double-helix form.

Opposite:
Jill Ergenbright photographed by Ric Ergenbright in 1975 in front of one of the three hundred *moai* statues on Easter Island, at Ahu Tahai, Chile. Discovered in 1722 by the Dutch sailor Jakob Roggeveen, these stone sculptures remain an enigma. What cult worshipped on this island?
To what gods are these giant *moais* an homage?
Why this size?
How were they erected?
A mystery. Restored, the *moai* presents itself with its cylindrical headdress, or *pukao*, and its coral and obsidian eyes.

Previous pages:
The Palacio d'Abraxas in Noisy-le-Grand, by Ricardo Bofill Levi. Constructed between 1978 and 1983, this complex groups nearly six hundred housing units in a U-shaped reinforced concrete structure and is a perfect example of postmodern style. Adherents of this trend borrow increasingly from the past, allowing antique columns and pediments to suddenly sprout. Everyone has a right to a palace.

Above:
A still from the James Bond film *You Only Live Twice*, directed by Lewis Gilbert, 1967. Discretion and notoriety don't mix well—except in fictional heroes, of whom Bond is the archetype. Killer of public enemies, lady killer, athlete, aesthete, he's the ideal man. Facing down power-hungry megalomaniacs is all in a day's work for Bond.

Opposite:
Model simulating the urban space of Fritz Lang's film *Metropolis*, attributed to Otto Hünte, Erich Kettelhut, and Karl Vollbrecht, 1926. As Lang's movie illustrates, the price of omnipotence is often total destruction. Inspired by the annihilation of Nero's ancient Rome, *Metropolis* seems to prefigure the ruin of Berlin in 1945.

Previous pages:
On July 1, 1982, at Madison Square Garden, in New York, the Reverend Sun Myung Moon married twenty-two thousand couples, members of his Unification Church. False sectarian prophets, visionaries, or divine incarnations? Gurus are everywhere, adored, adulated, and financed by the crowds.

Above:
Citizen Kane, directed by and starring Orson Welles, 1941. With a revolutionary screenplay by Welles and Herman Mankiewicz, this mythic film recounts the story of an extraordinary character, a media tycoon who dies in his unfinished mansion, Xanadu, just after having uttered the enigmatic word: "Rosebud." *Citizen Kane* represents the meeting of an important movie personage with a cinematic master not far removed from his character.

Opposite:
Michael Anderson's *1984*, starring Edmond O'Brien (1956). An adaptation of the 1949 novel by George Orwell, the film depicts a totalitarian state inspired by both Nazism and Stalinism. A premonitory work, it is famous for the phrase "Big Brother is watching you," foreshadowing our society of surveillance and widespread indoctrination. For dictators around the world, this Big Brother is a brother indeed.

A scene from Stanley Kubrick's *Dr. Strangelove, Or How I Learned to Stop Worrying and Love the Bomb*, starring Peter Sellers (1964). Nearly twenty years after dropping two atomic bombs on the Japanese cities of Hiroshima and Nagasaki, the cold war rages between the United States and the Soviet Union. This film denounces, in a zany and hysterical manner, the growing arms race. Following a transmission error, the Americans, believing they are under attack, set the counterstrike in motion, but cannot put a stop to it once they've realized their mistake. Because it now has the means to destroy the Earth, the human race is doomed by its own power.

Construction site of the Aswan Dam,
constructed between 1898 and 1902.
Built by the British to reach up to the first
of the Nile's six cataracts, the first dam
led to the submersion of Lower Nubia.
Because flooding and droughts posed
a constant threat to Egypt's cotton fields,
it was enlarged and strengthened twice.
In the 1970s, a second dam was
constructed with the aid of the Soviets,
who were anxious to cement their
friendship with President Gamal
Abdel Nasser's Egypt. In order for this
construction to take place, it was
necessary to shift around several
archaeological sites along the Nile.
We now know the disastrous ecological
consequences of this enormous project.

Above:
French Spiderman Alain Robert, scaling the Abu Dhabi Investment Authority Tower, 2007.
Others, just as famous, have resorted to suction cups, hooks, cords; Robert uses only his ten fingers and
a pair of shoes with nonslip soles. With these simple tools he has climbed more than seventy large-scale
buildings around the world, eluding the authorities, security guards, and police. Normally, his pursuers
can do nothing but wait for him at the top of the buildings. How could they catch this devilish man,
capable of clinging to the vertical facades of skyscrapers?

Opposite:
Tightrope walker Philippe Petit maneuvers between the towers of Notre Dame Cathedral in Paris,
June 1971. One sees only him, an angel floating among the cathedral's gargoyles. The wind blowing,
he balances himself accordingly, infinitesimal, yet immense. On the rope that he grazes with the soles
of his feet, he is the embodiment of gracefulness, yet this absolute grace flaunts itself as a form of defiance.
It is megalomania at work—the possibility of falling being the only drawback.

This page and following pages:
Moscow Millionaires' salon, 2007. Moscow, with approximately sixty thousand millionaires,
has become the most profitable city in the world for investors.
Here, social success is paraded without restraint. Luxury villas, cars, diamonds,
supermodels, and private airplanes are only the tip of the iceberg.

ДА ЗДРАВСТВУЕТ ВЕ
КОММУНИСТИЧЕСКОЙ П
ТОВАРИЩ

Previous pages:
The Rolling Stones performing at Chicago's Soldier Field Stadium during their "Bridges to Babylon" tour, 1997.
Photograph by Brian Rasic. For nearly half a century, Mick Jagger and his band have electrified crowds.
Escorted in via helicopter, stirring the bowels of the earth, dazzling tens of millions of fans with flickering
spotlights, spattering cities with their images, their faces, their logo, on posters or flat screens, the Stones,
like all rock giants, are stars whose presence the explosion of technologies has made all the more ubiquitous.

Above:
Homage to Joseph Stalin, whose seventieth birthday was celebrated at the Bolshoi Theater in Moscow in 1950 by a spectacular cast of characters. From left to right: Palmiro Togliatti, Semyon Budenny, Lazar Kaganovich, Mikhail Suslov, Mao Tse-tung, Nikolai Bulganin, Joseph Stalin, Alexandr Vasilevsky, Nikita Khrushchev, Dolores Ibárruri, Gheorghe Gheorghiu-Dej, Nikolay Shvernik, Georgy Malenkov, Lavrenty Beria, Kliment Voroshilov, Vyacheslav Molotov, and Artem Mikoyan—more than one of these dictators, elites, and revolutionaries was executed shortly thereafter by Stalin's compatriots.

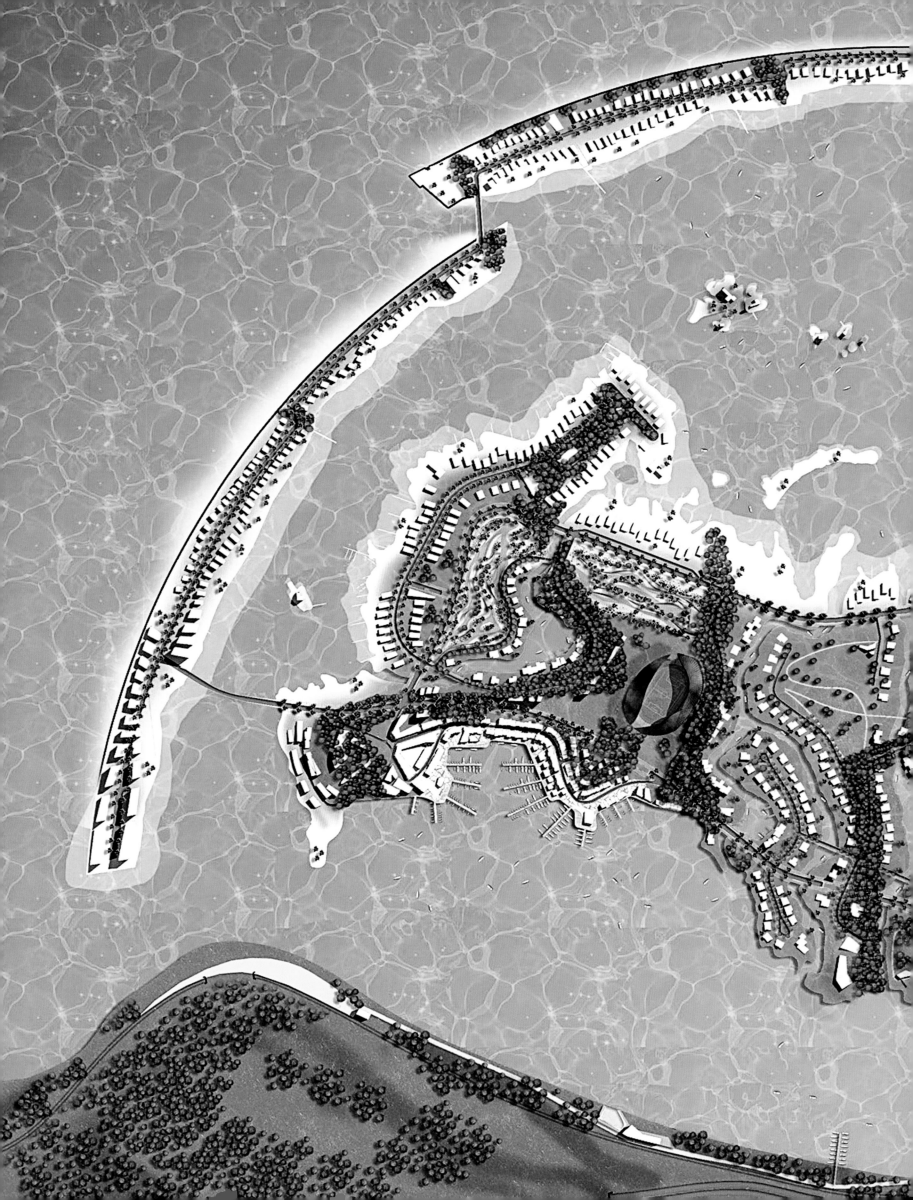

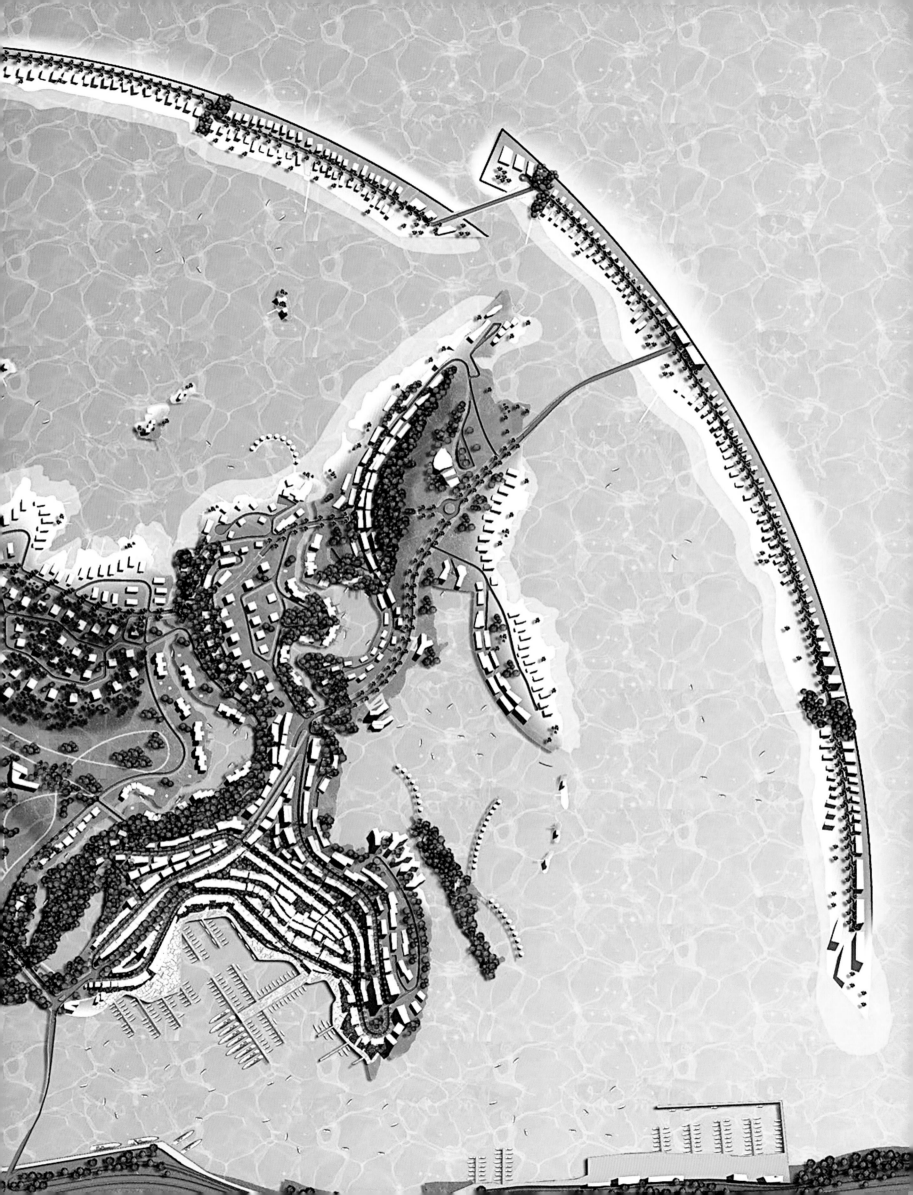

Previous pages:
Federation Island, an 815-acre artificial island to be constructed on the Black Sea.
Designed by Dutch architect Erick van Egeraat in the shape of Russia,
it will accommodate twenty-five thousand people for the 2014 Olympics.

Opposite:
Ugandan president Idi Amin Dada in 1979 in Dijon, A collage by Roland-Paul Gudin
made from boxes of expired medicines. Here, the African dictator is ready to devour
his former tutelary state, Great Britain. It says much about the violence that still rocks
the nations born from the march to independence in the 1960s and alludes
to the popular conviction that Amin Dada was secretly a cannibal.

Following pages:
The Sans-Souci Palace in Haiti, photographed by Roloff Beny. Henri Christophe, a former
slave turned army general, became the first black king of Haiti. Crowning himself Henri I in 1811,
he ordered the construction of this palace with the hopes of rivaling the one at Versailles.
He opted for a prerevolutionary French architectural style, with obelisks, Doric columns,
and pyramids; the outcome is a composite of Greek and Egyptian allusions. Situated in the town of
Milot, below the Citadelle Laferrière, the palace stretches out over more than eight hilly hectares.
The palace's walls were covered with mahogany sculptures; its marble floors cooled by a mountain
stream that ran below. The Sans-Souci Palace was looted after King Henri's 1820 suicide.
Megalomaniac to the end, the monarch shot himself in the forehead with a golden bullet.

Opposite:
Castle of King Ludwig II of Bavaria in Neuschwanstein, Germany. The castle served as a model
for that of Walt Disney's *Sleeping Beauty*. Decried during its construction, this eccentric whim
littered with turrets and supported by walls of loose stones has become the most famous castle
in the Bavarian Alps. Its builder, a friend of the bombastic composer Richard Wagner, had
conceived it after visiting the Château de Pierrefonds in France, reconstructed by Viollet-le-Duc.
Consumed with caprices and indifferent to the affairs of his kingdom, Ludwig II ended up
ruining his finances and losing his popularity. His castle remains unfinished.

Following pages:
View of Michael Jackson's personal amusement park, Neverland Ranch, near Santa Ynez,
California. Rock stars, movie stars, soccer stars, and race-car drivers live cut off from the public
in their tucked-away palaces. Nothing is too grandiose to complement their success:
sports-car collections, paintings, wild animals, multiple marriages, scandals…
Making the front page is essential, even if their celebrity depends on a certain distance
between themselves and their public.

Previous pages:
The Camp de Boulogne, laid out under the orders of Napoleon I on August 15, 1804. Resolved to invade England, the emperor had an enormous camp built at the port in Boulogne. More than 150,000 soldiers were assembled, and it is there that, on August 16, 1804, Napoleon organized a ceremony to award, for the first time, the decorations of the Légion d'Honneur. The celebration lasted seven hours but fired imaginations for many more.

Opposite:
A scene from the film *The Great Dictator*, directed by and starring Charlie Chaplin (1940). Chaplin plays Adenoid Hynkel here, a dictator ruling the fictional country of Tomania. Confronted with the bloody dictatorship of Adolf Hitler, Chaplin found refuge in the comic and the outrageous. Through his role, he ridicules all the traits of criminal megalomania: paranoid gesticulations, cries, tics, threatening barks, grins, swaggering…nothing escapes his scornful scrutiny. The tables are turned when Chaplin's other character, Charlot, the buffoon, becomes a legend himself.

PHOTO CREDITS

p. 16–17: © Imaginechina/ICC/AFP; p. 18–19: © Richard Soberka – www.photoway.com; p. 20: © Paris – Musée de l'Armée, Dist. RMN/Pascal Segrette; p. 21: © Stephen Stickler/Corbis; p. 22–23: © Larry Towell/Magnum Photos; p. 25: © Cavalcade/RM Films International/The Kobal Collection; p. 26–27: © Mark Power/Magnum Photos; p. 28–29: © Petar Kujundzic/Pool/AFP; p.30–31: © Patrick Robert/Sygma/Corbis; p. 32–33: © Richard Soberka – www.photoway.com; p. 34: © Ferdinando Scianna/Magnum Photos; p. 35: © Rene Burri/Magnum Photos; p. 36–37: © Christo, 1970, photo © Harry Shunk; p. 38–39: © Jorge Ferrari/EPA/Corbis; p. 40–41: © Xinhua/AFP; p. 42–43: © Yann Arthus-Bertrand/Altitude; p. 44: © BPK, Berlin, Dist RMN/Volker-H. Schneider; p. 45: © EMAAR Properties/AFP; p. 46–47: © NASA/Getty Images; p. 49: © Sylvie Chappaz/www.vandystadt.com/ Agence Regards du sport; p. 50–51: © Alain Nogues/Corbis; p. 52: © Bettmann/Corbis; p. 53: © Mary Evans Picture Library 2006/Rue des Archives; p. 54–55: © Massimo Listri/Corbis; p. 56–57: © Wark Producing Company/The Kobal Collection; p. 58–59: © Richard Soberka – www.photoway.com; p. 61: © Bettmann/Corbis; p. 62 left: © Foster and Partners, right: © Mori Building Co./Getty Images/AFP; p. 63 left: © Fordham Company/Getty Images/AFP, right: © Tobu Railway/Getty Images/AFP; p. 65: © Photononstop/AFP; p. 67: © Elliott Erwitt/Magnum Photos; p. 68–69: © EPA/Corbis; p. 70: © Jose Fuste Raga/Corbis; p. 71: © The Japan Architect Co., Ltd, photo © Shinkenchiku-Sha; p. 72–73: © David Hurn/Magnum Photos; p. 74–75: © Thomas Hoepker/Magnum Photos; p. 76: © Schusev State Museum of Architecture, Moscow; p. 77: © Owaki-Kulla/Corbis; p. 78–79: © Gavin Hellier/Robert Harding World Imagery/Corbis; p. 80–81: © Fondation Le Corbusier/ADAGP, Paris, 2008; p. 83: © George Hammerstein/Solus-Veer/Corbis; p. 84–85: © Miroslav Zajíc/Corbis; p. 86: © Orlan, photo © CNAC/MNAM, Dist. RMN/Philippe Migeat; p. 87: © ADAGP, Paris, 2008, photo © Andy Warhol Foundation for the Visual Arts/Corbis; p. 88–89: © Patrick Mimran; p. 90–91: © Jeremy Horner/Corbis; p. 92–93: © Bettmann/Corbis; p. 94–95: © ADAGP, Paris, 2008; p. 97: © Catherine Field/AFP; p. 98–99: © Sarai Suarez/EPA/Corbis; p. 100: © Patrick Durand/Corbis Sygma; p. 101: © Guy Le Querrec/Magnum Photos; p. 102–103: © Akg-Images; p. 104: © 2008 Photo Smithsonian American Art Museum/Art Resource/Scala, Florence; p. 105: © Louie Psihoyos/Corbis; p. 106: © ADAGP, Paris, 2008, photo © CNAC/MNAM, Dist. RMN/Jacques Faujour; p. 107: © Ric Ergenbright/Corbis; p. 108–109: © Collection Artedia; p. 110: © Rue des Archives/BCA; p. 111: © The Kobal Collection/UFA; p. 112–113: © Bettmann/Corbis; p. 114: © Rue des Archives/BCA; p. 115: © The Kobal Collection/Columbia; p. 116–117: © Rue des Archives/BCA; p. 118–119: © Hulton-Deutsch Collection/Corbis; p. 120: © STR/AFP; p. 121: © STF/AFP; p. 122–123: © Dmitry Kostyukov/AFP; p. 124–125: © Denis Sinyakov/AFP; p. 126–127: © Brian Rasic; p. 128–129: © Bettmann/Corbis; p. 130–131: © Handout/AFP; p. 133: © AFP; p. 134–135: © Roloff Beny/Bibliothèque et Archives Canada; p. 137: © Library of Congress; p. 138–139: © Justin Sullivan/Getty Images/AFP; p. 140–141: © The Art Archive/ Napoleonic Museum Rome/Dagli Orti; p. 143: © Bettmann/Corbis.

ACKNOWLEDGMENTS

The editors would like to thank first of all Frédérique Sarfati Romano, without whom this project would not have been possible, as well as Véronique Ristelhueber.

Additionally, we would like to thank the photographers and artists who participated in this work, especially Christo and Jeanne-Claude, Patrick Mimran, Orlan, Brian Rasic, and Richard Soberka.

Finally, thank you to everyone who was involved in the graphic production of this work:
Morgane Balitrand and Valérie Lefèvre (AKG Images), Valentina Bandelloni (Scala Group), Eva Bodinet (Magnum Photos), Françoise Carminati and Fabienne Delfour (Corbis), Jok Church, Dalloula (Artedia), Elsa Franklin, Véronique Garrigues (Adagp), Isabelle Godineau (Fondation Le Corbusier), Carmen Hugue (Ricardo Boffill), Laurence Isabey (Getty Images), Sawa Kato (The Japan Architect Co., Ltd), Laurence Kersuzan and Pierrick Jan (RMN), Isabelle Lechenet (Agence Altitude), Anne Lorré (AFP), Daniel Potvin (Bibliothèque et Archives Canada), Lise Seguin and Lilia Mhedhbi (The Picture Desk), Catherine Terk (Rue des Archives), Kathryn Tollervey (Foster and Partners), and Gérard Vandystadt (Agence Regards du Sport).

[MEGAL

n., 1865, fro

mégalo-   a

Overestima

physical or m

of one's pow

delusions of g